FORM
SCENERY SEEN THROUGH BONSAI

RYO OHWADA

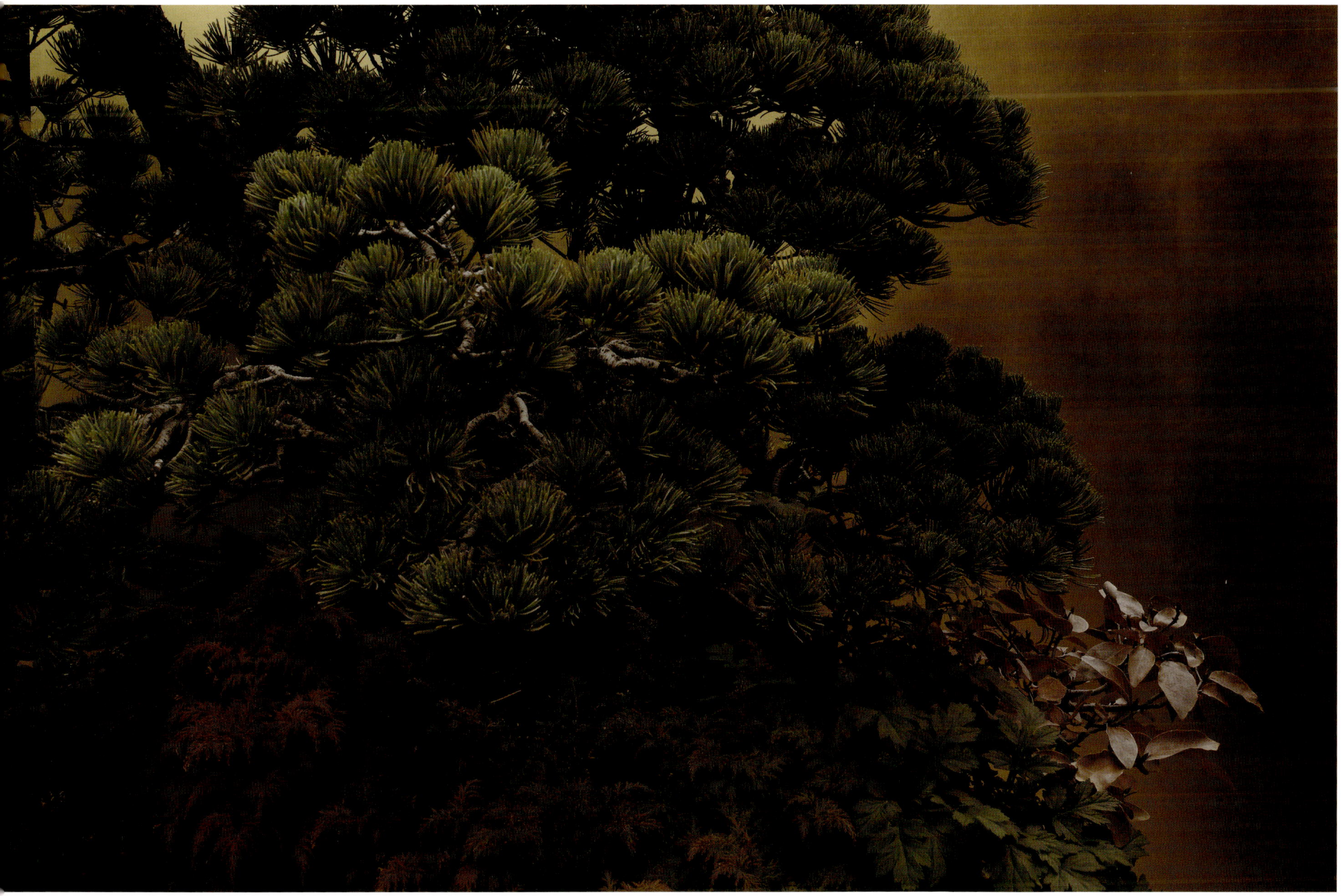

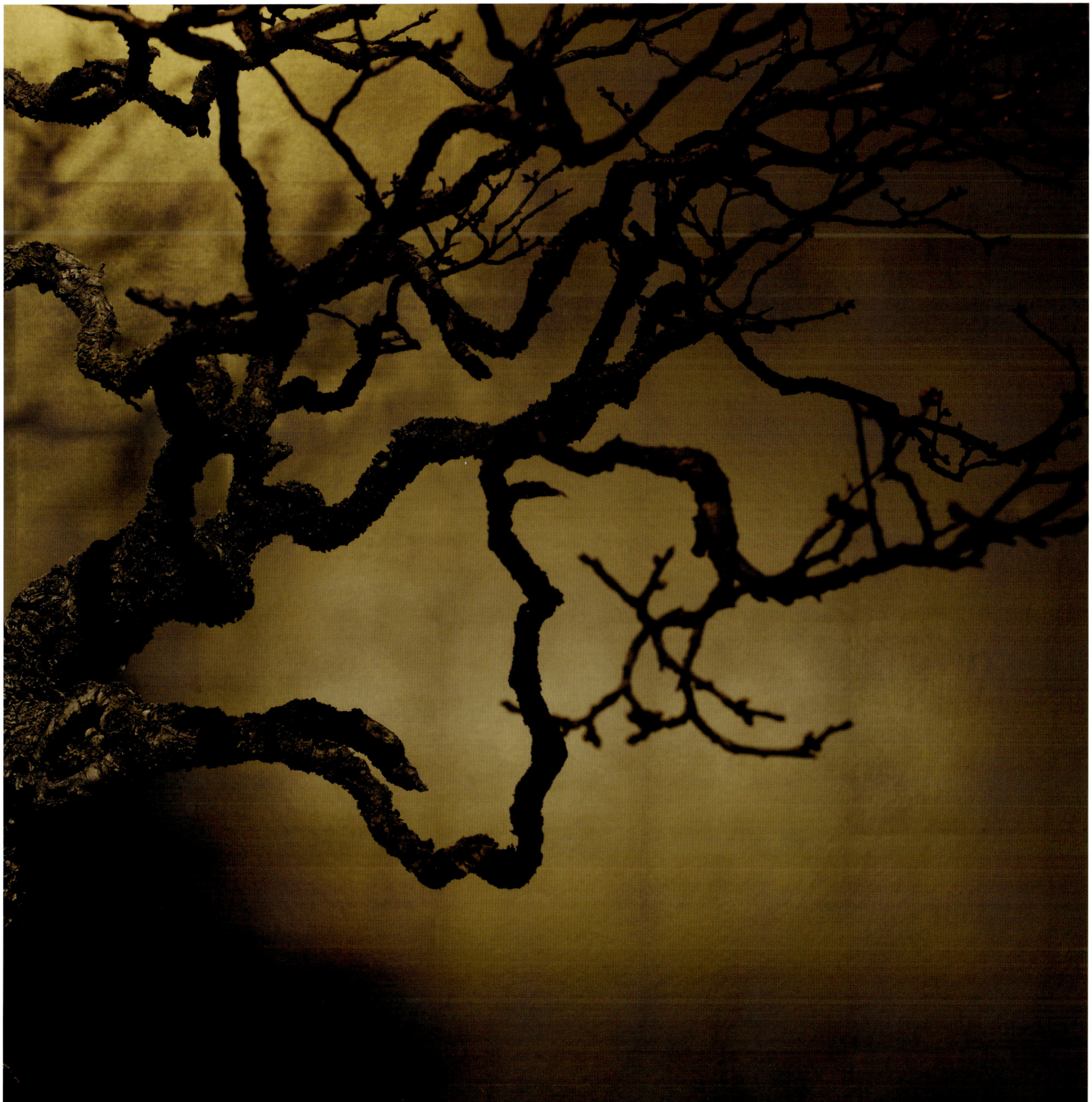

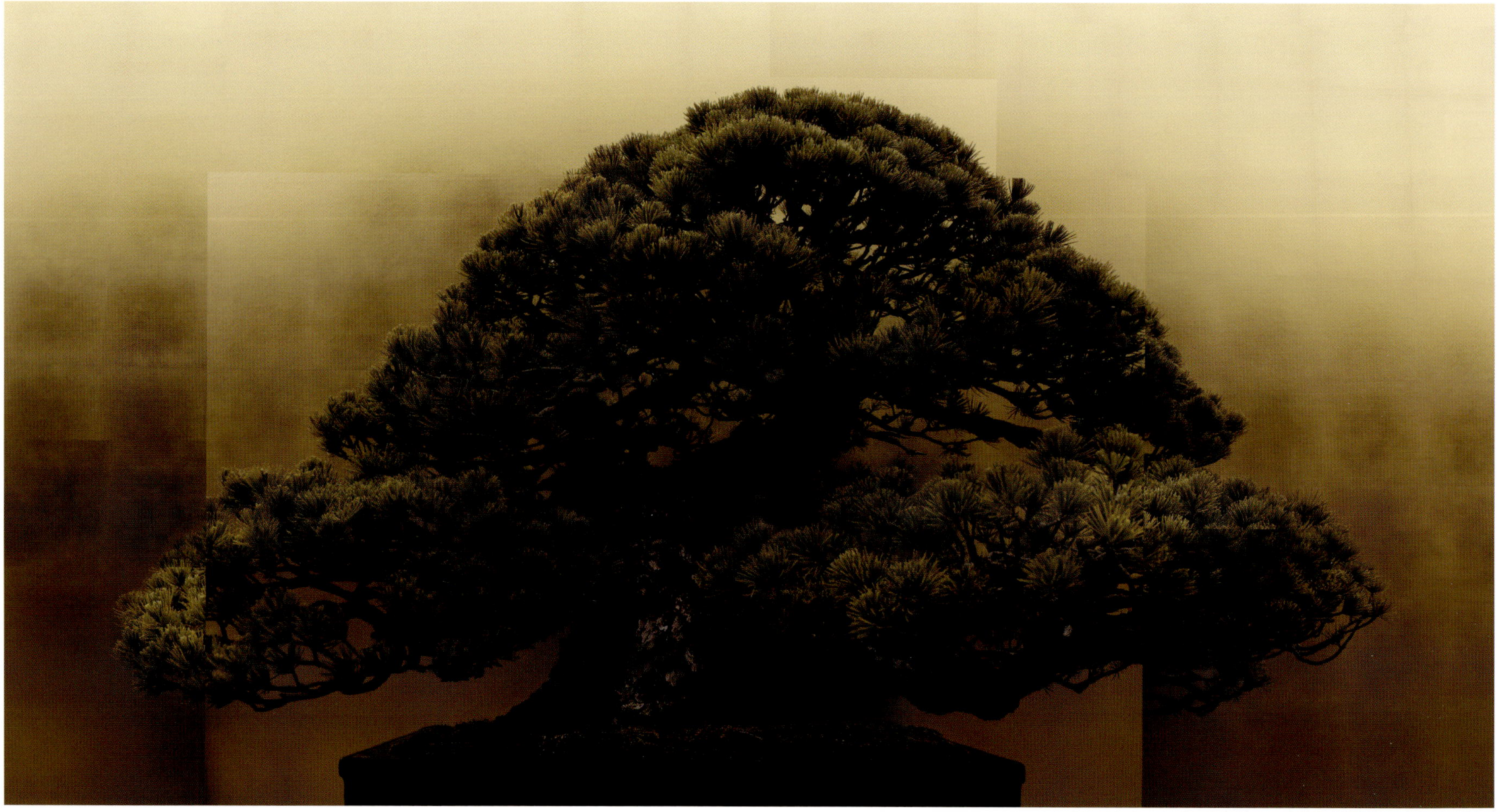

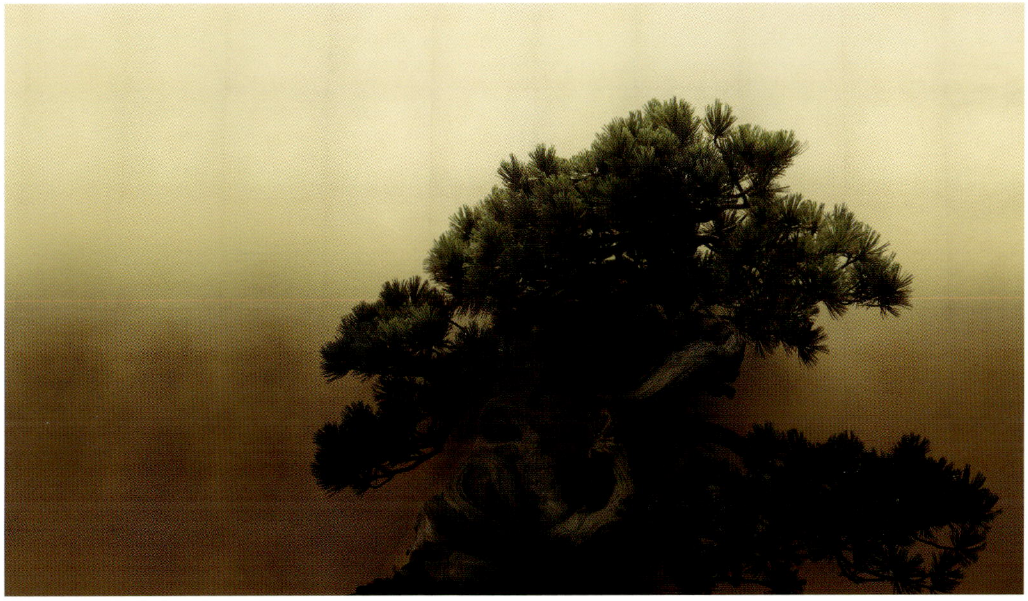

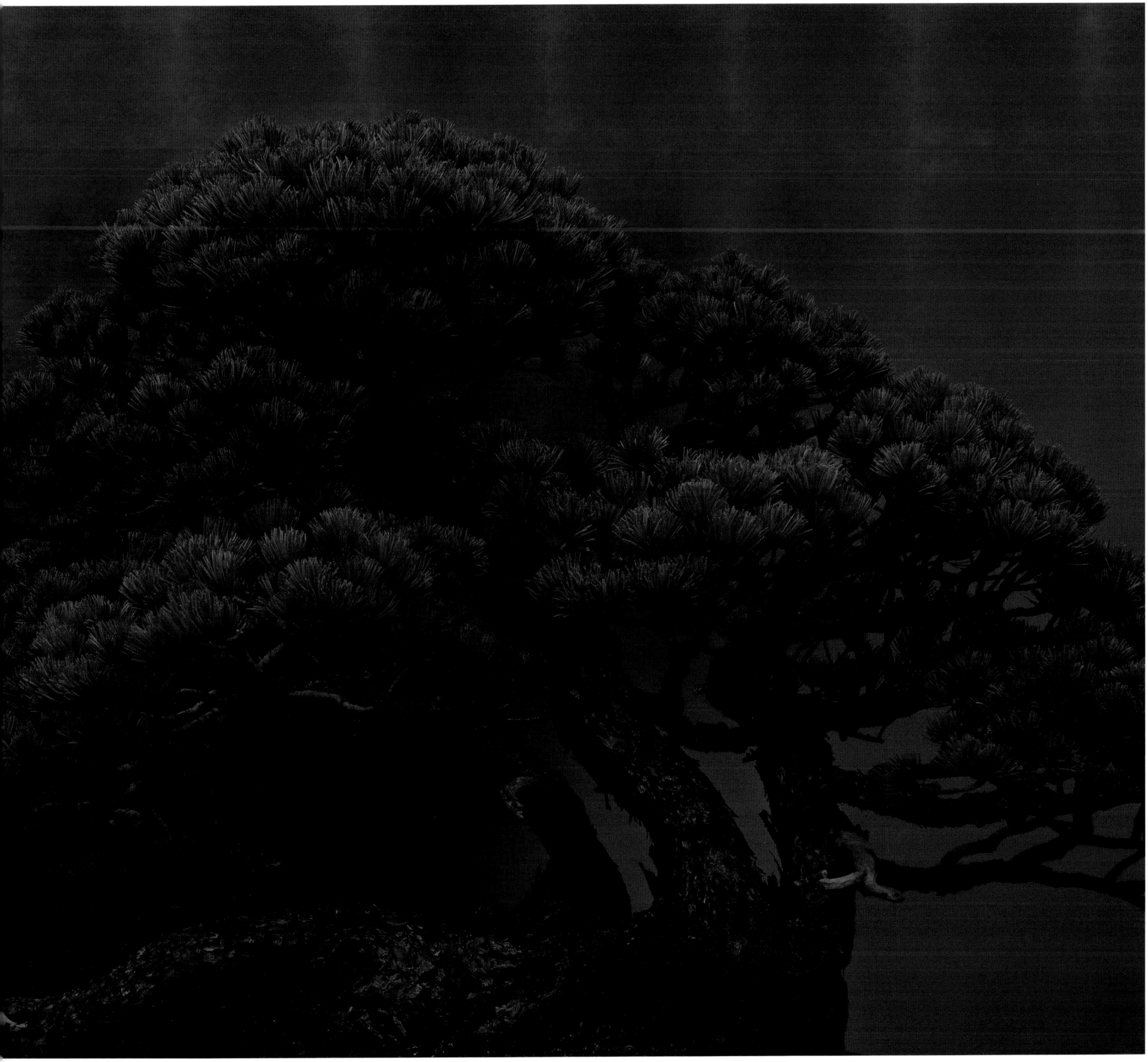

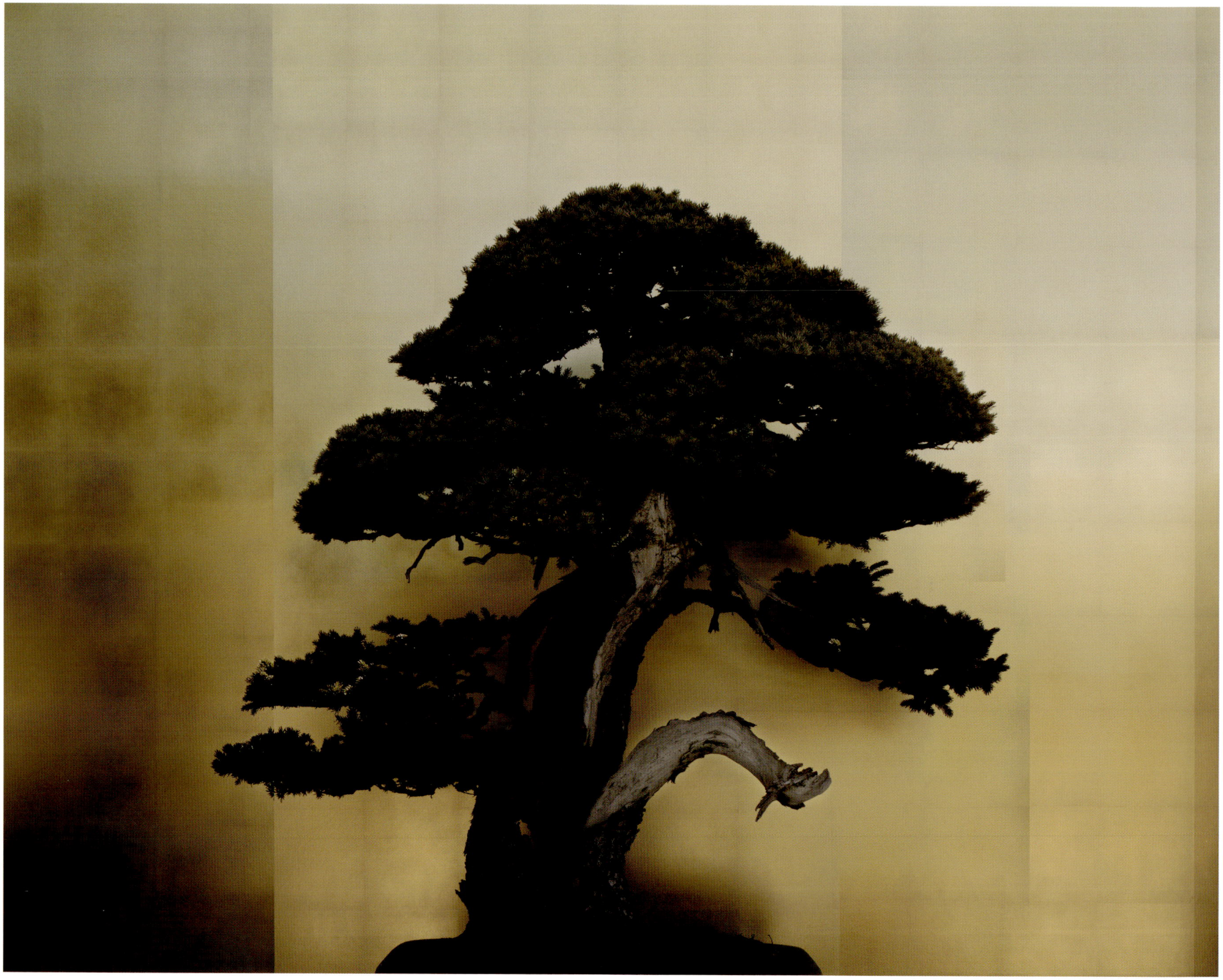

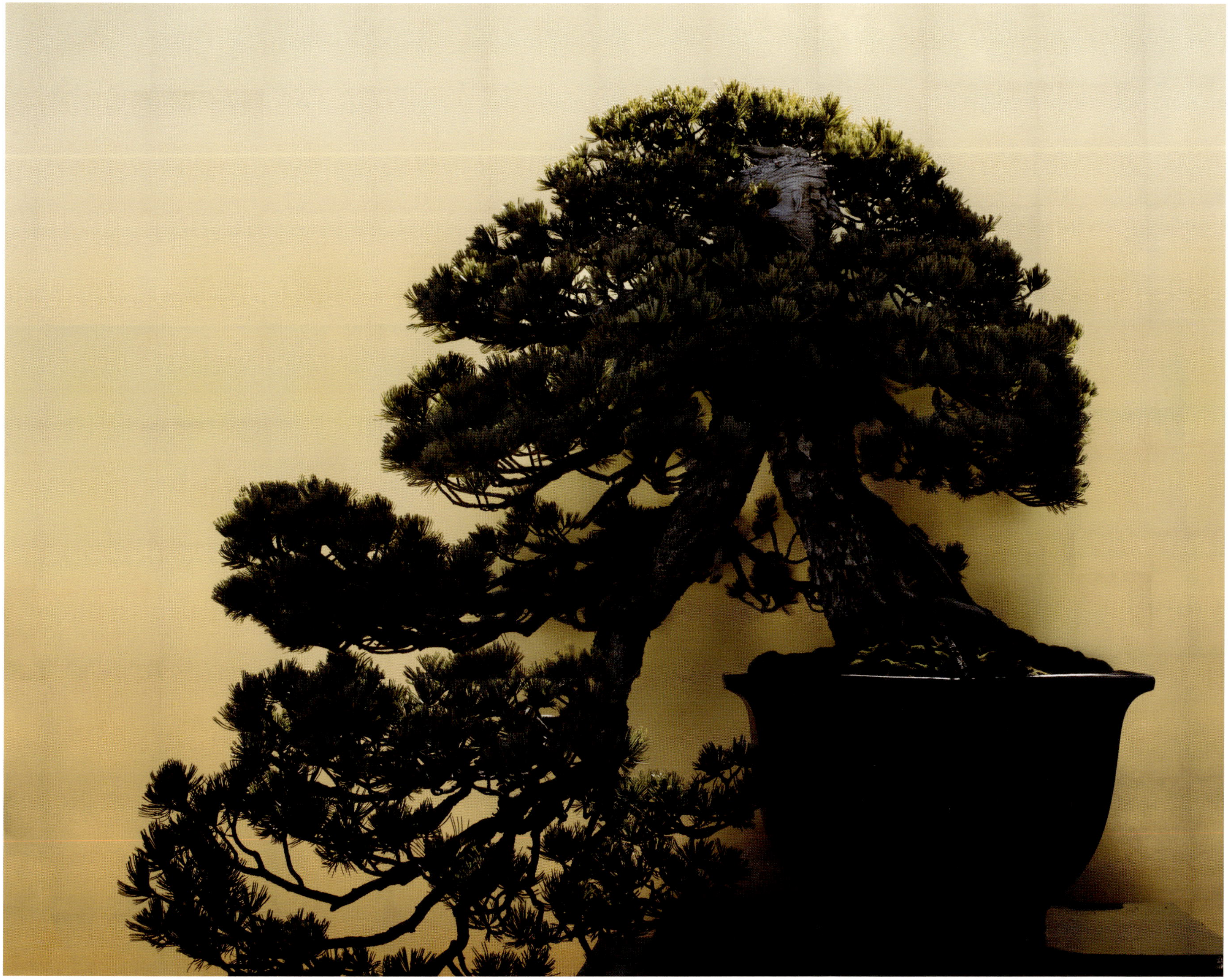

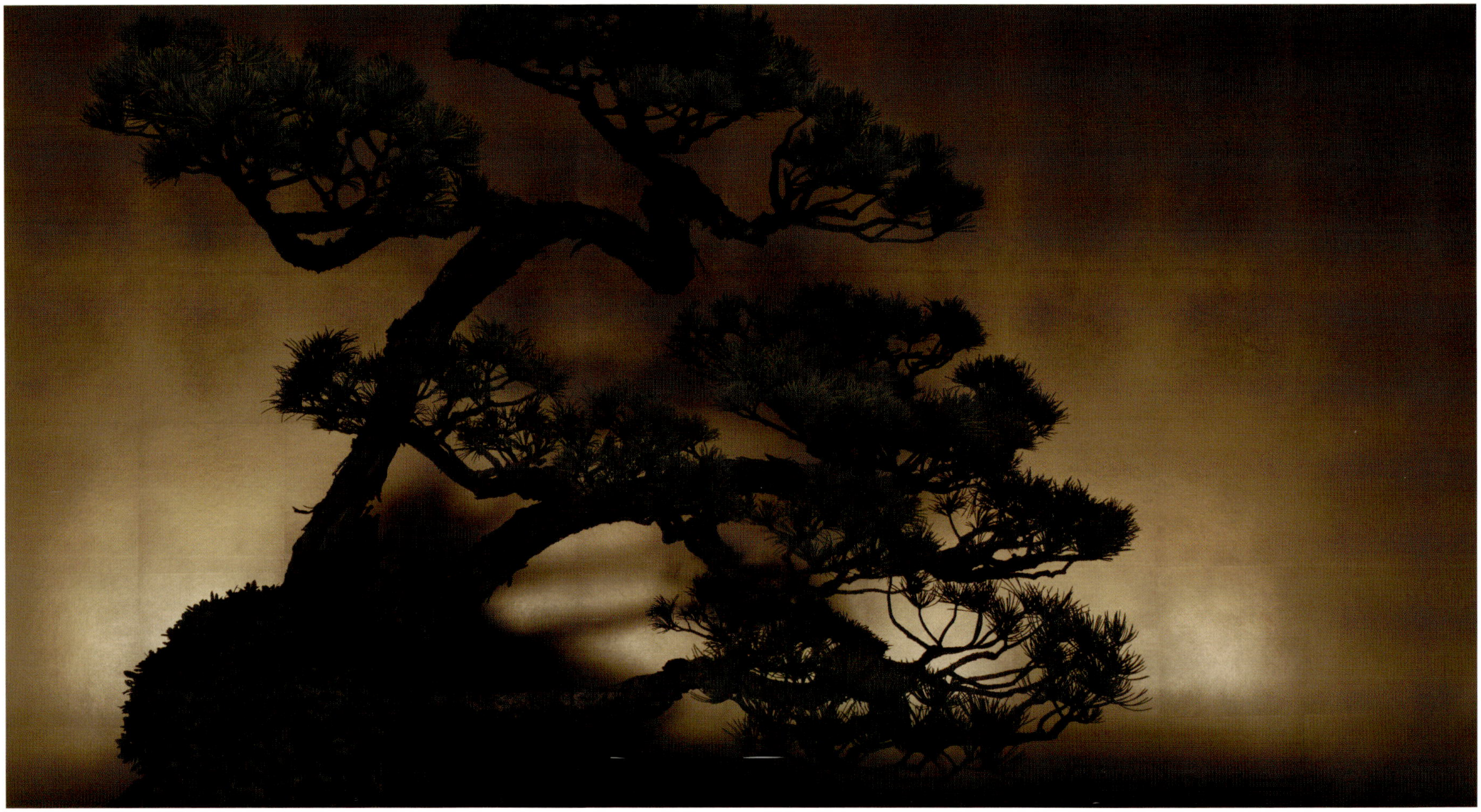

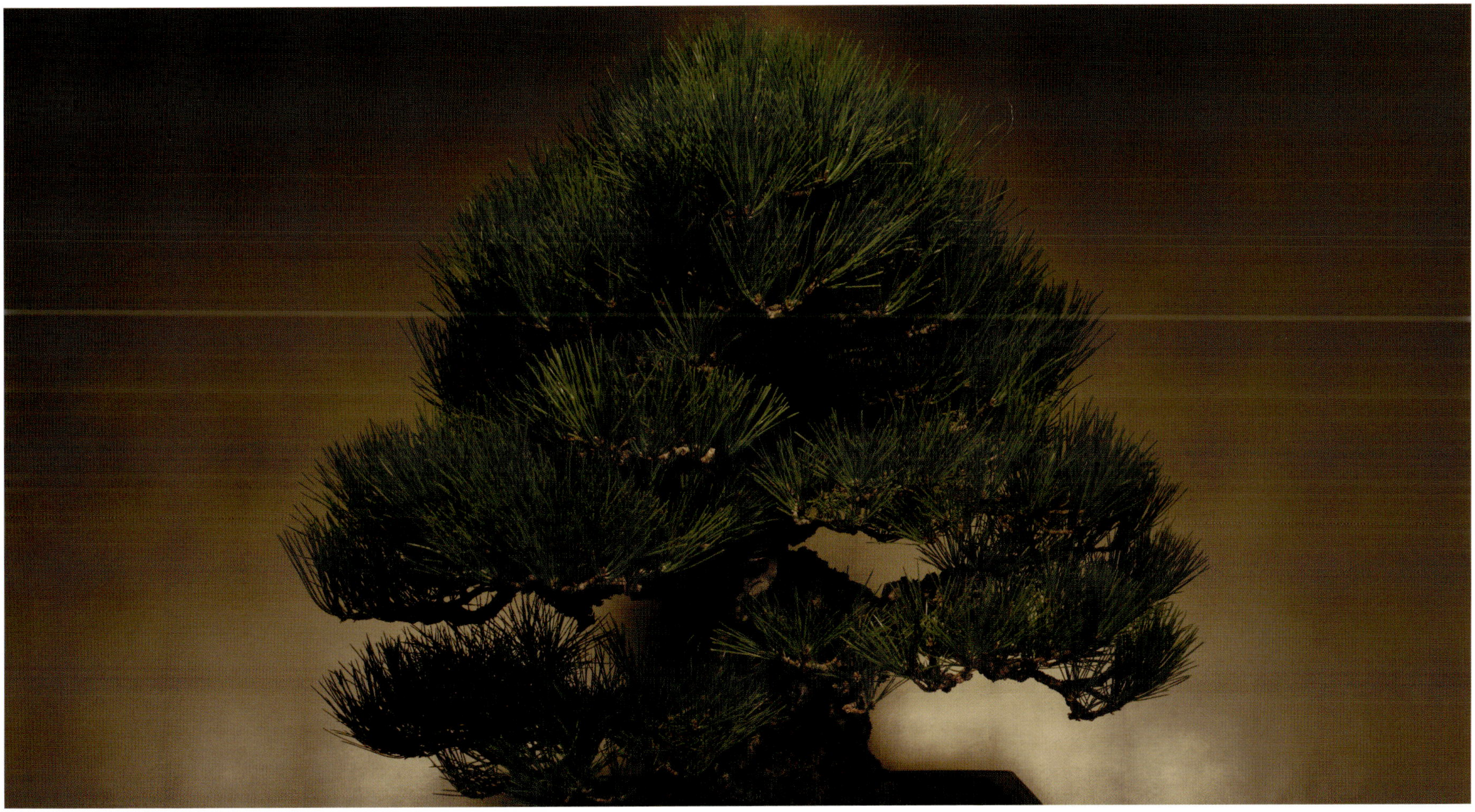

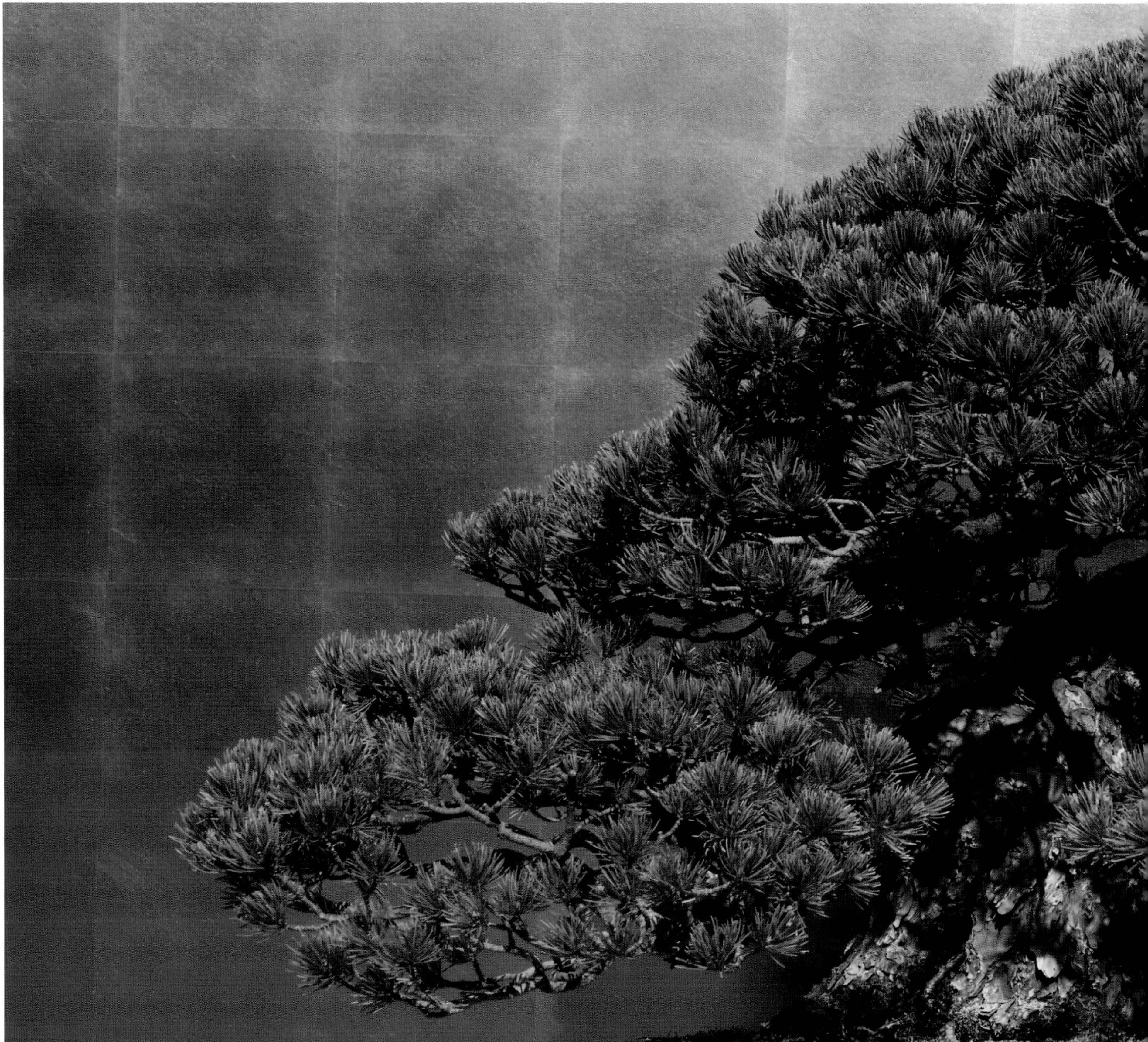

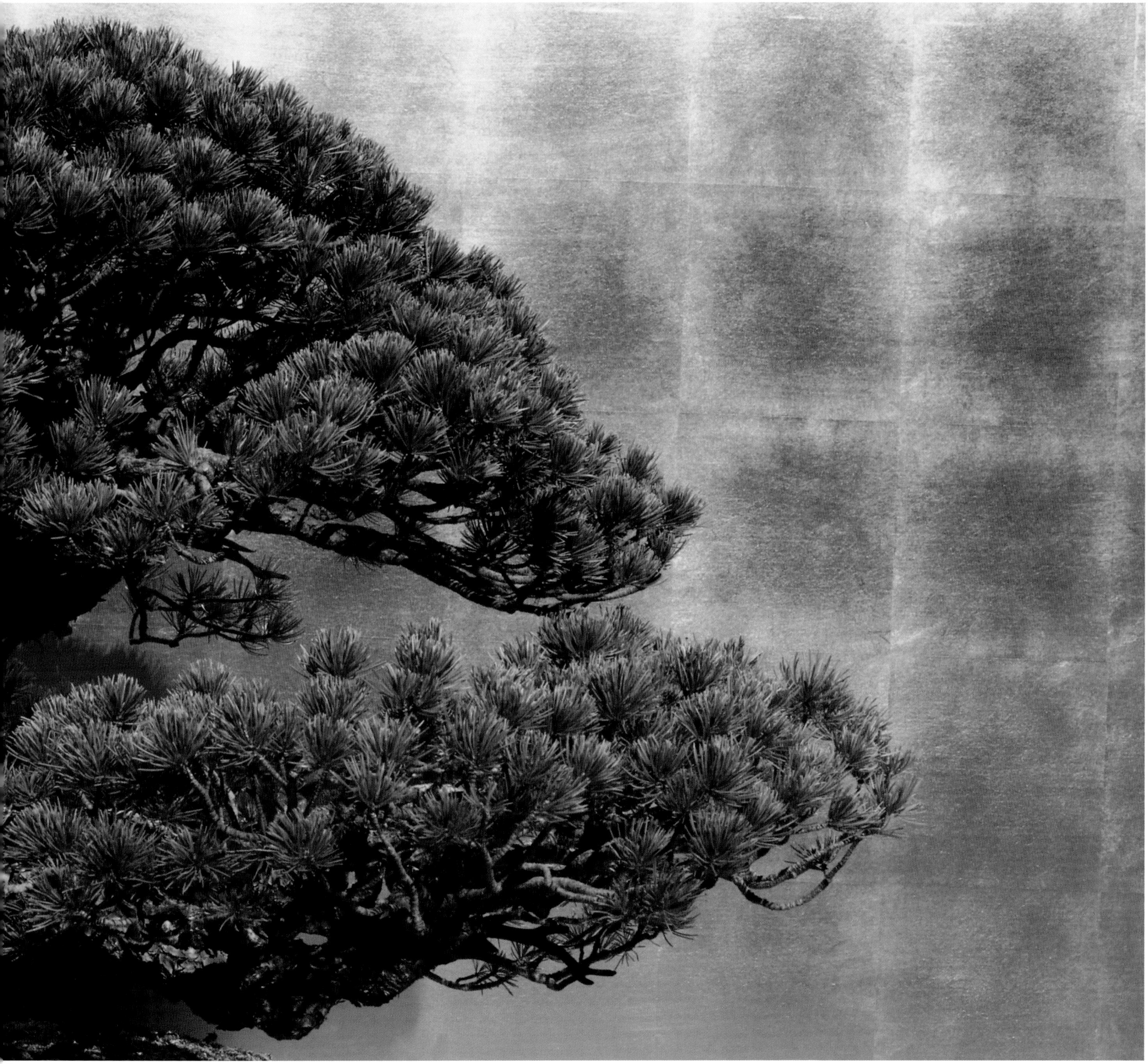

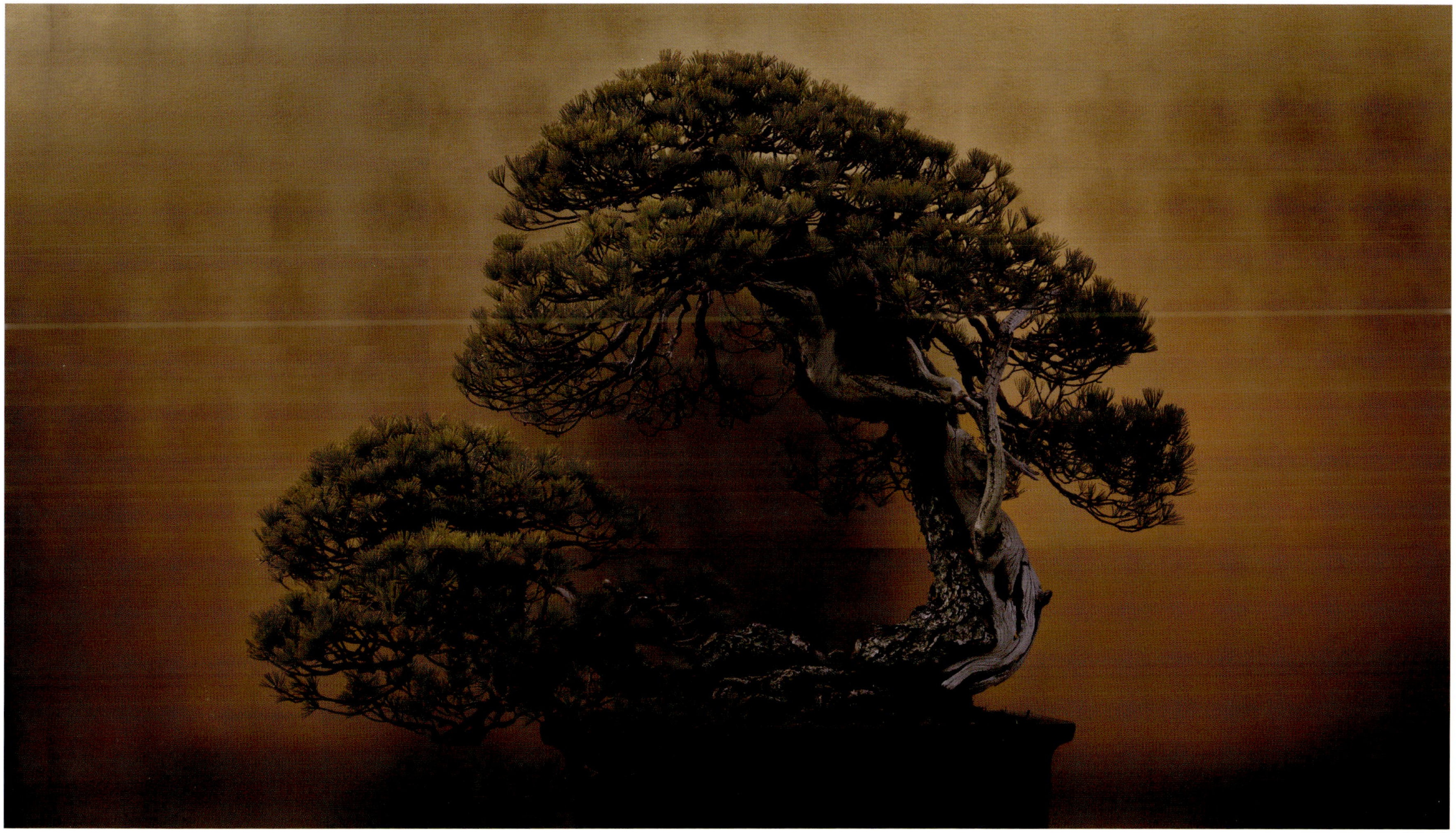

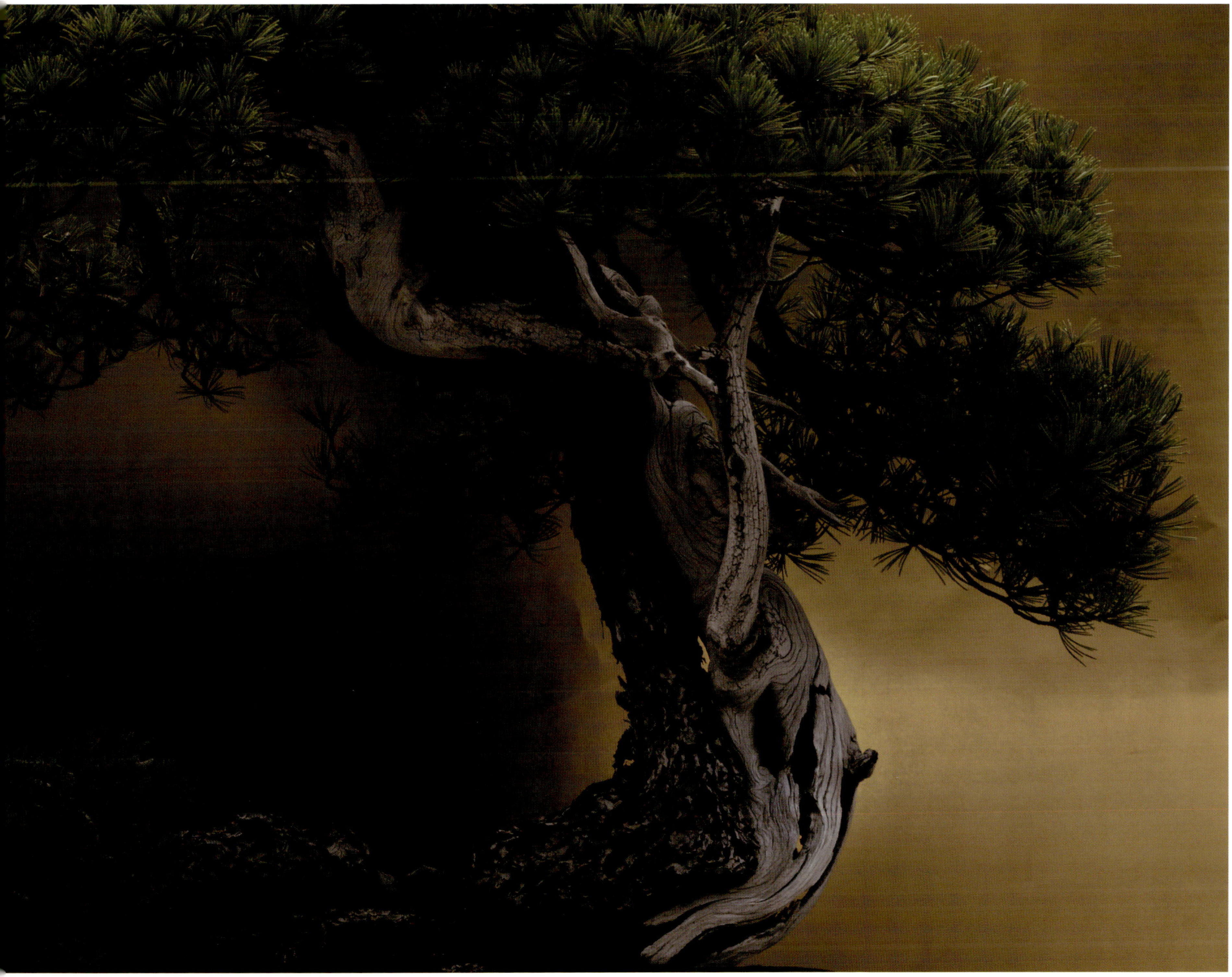

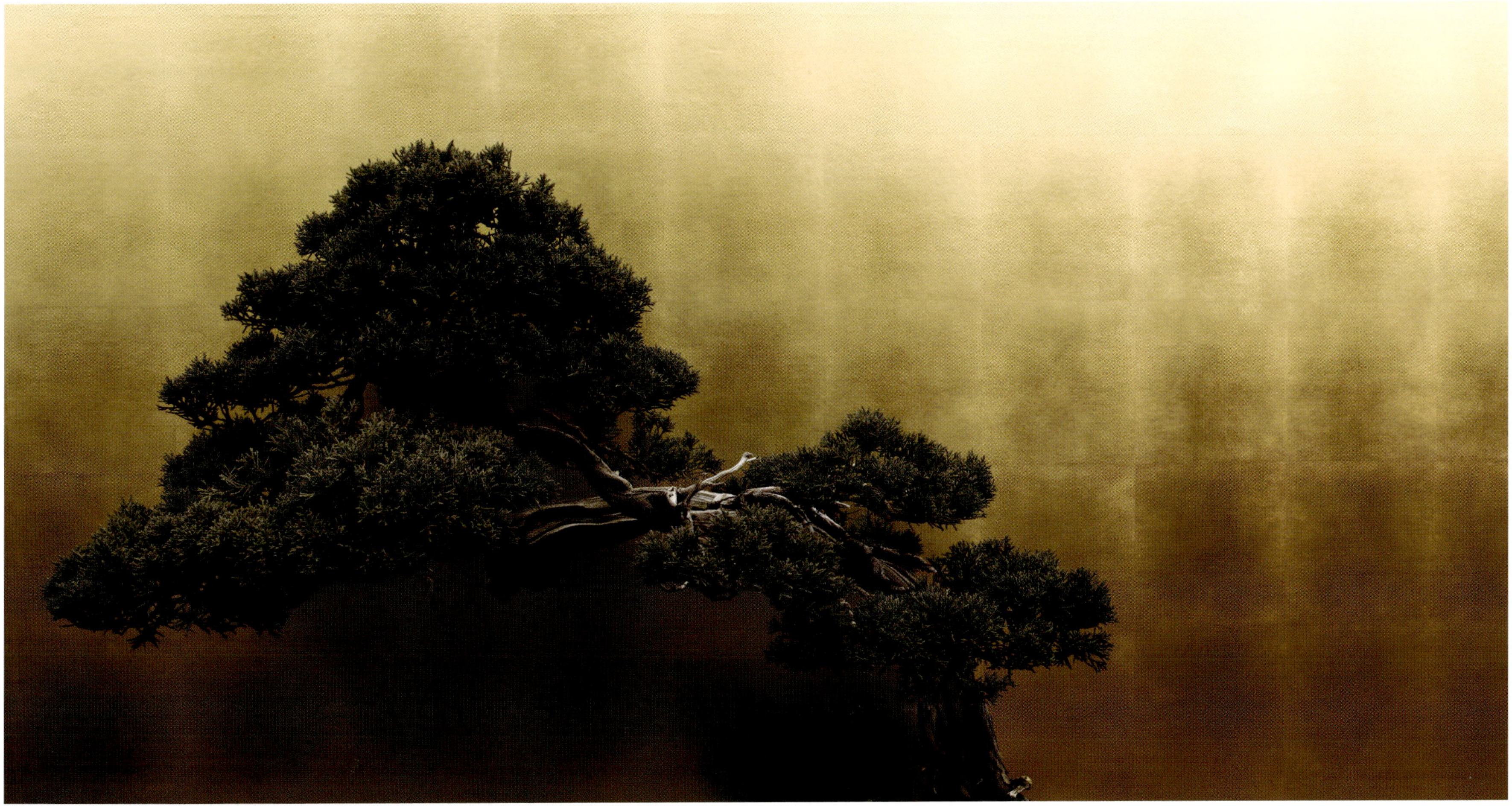

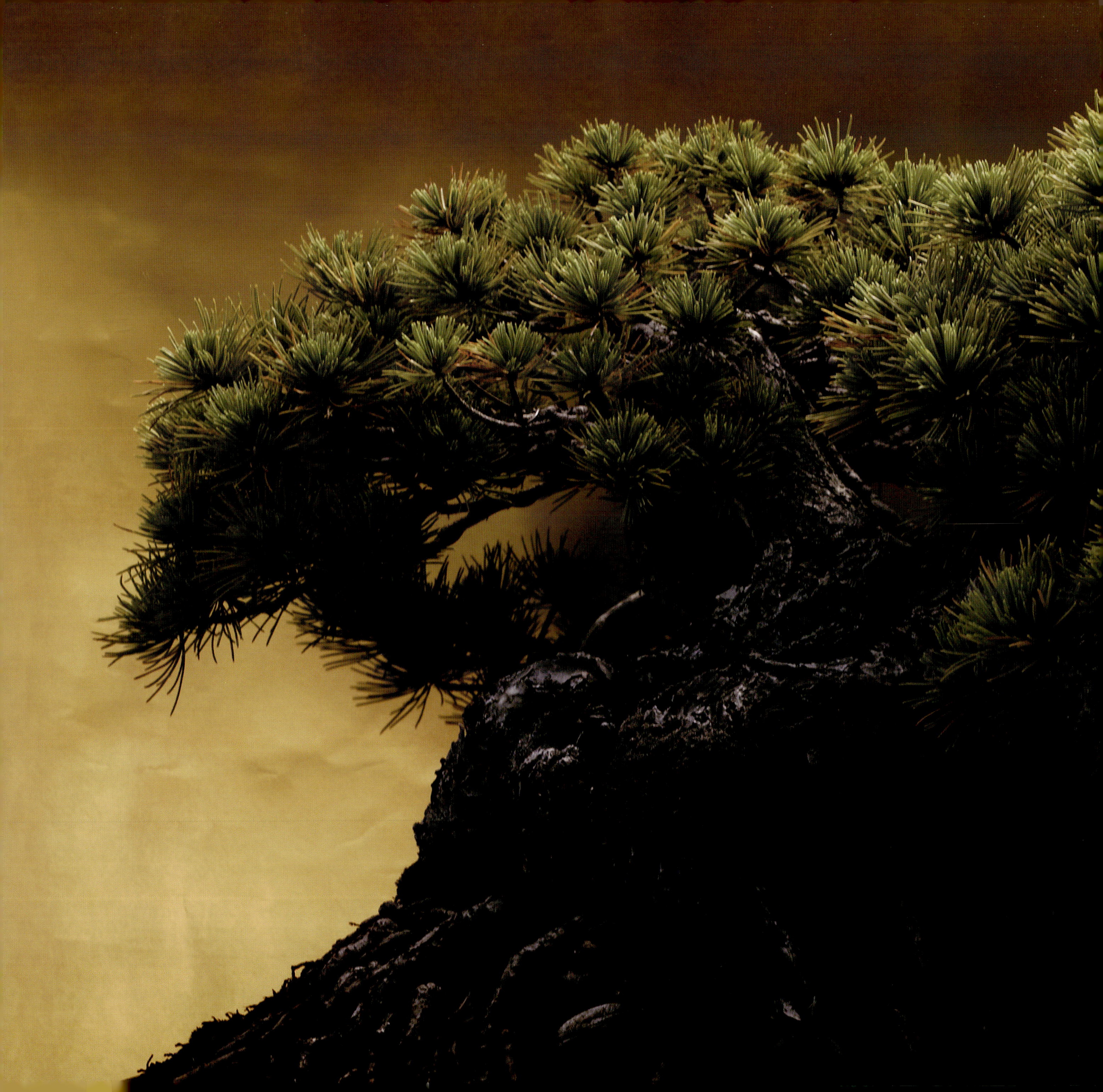

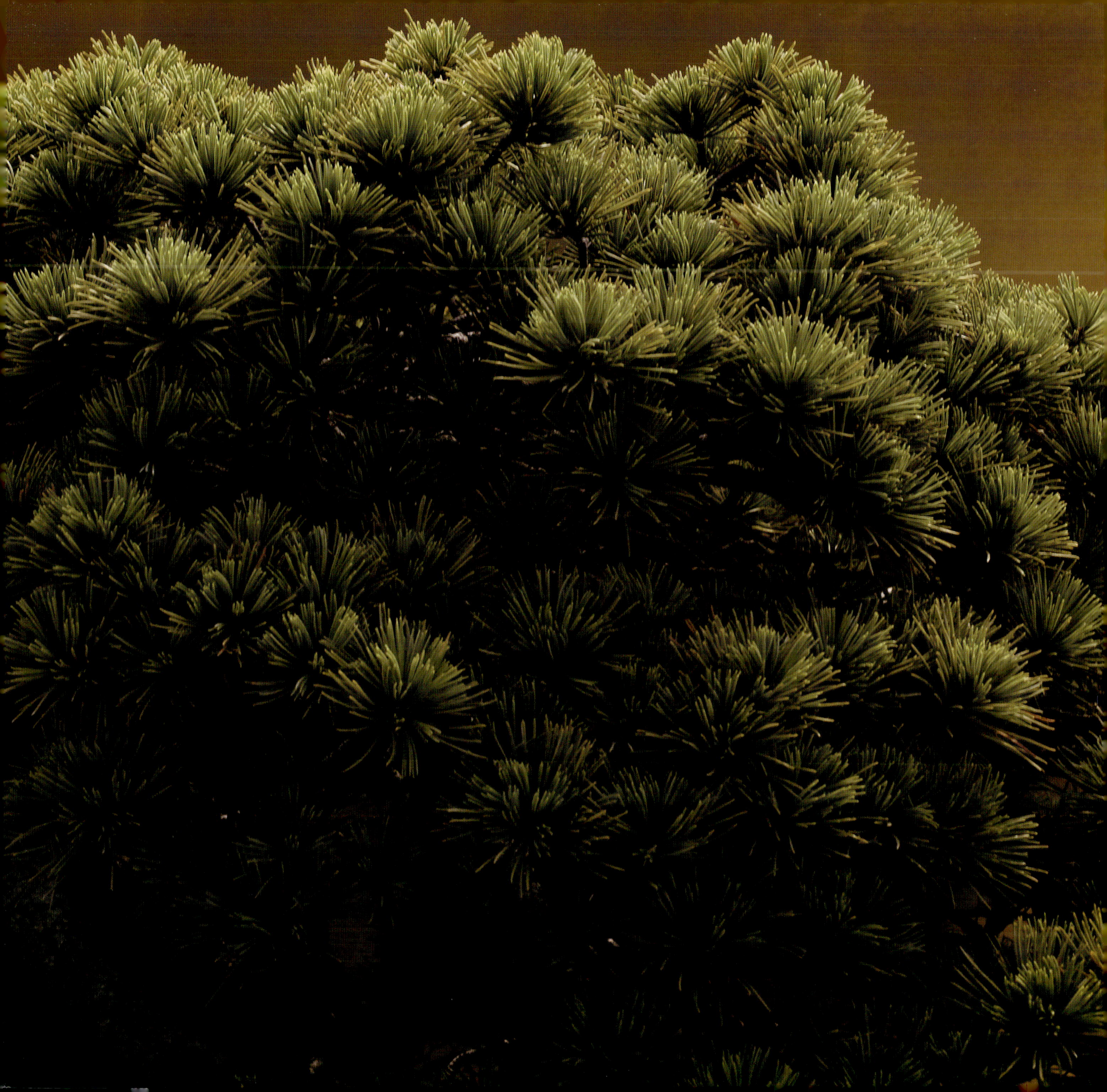

FORM
SCENERY SEEN THROUGH BONSAI

RYO OHWADA

強靭なる構成主義的琳派 ― 大和田良の新たな「盆栽写真」の誕生

大熊 敏之　富山大学大学院芸術文化学研究科准教授　前さいたま市大宮盆栽美術館館長

写真は、あくまでも写真であって、美術ではない。写真と絵画は、まったく別種の視覚表現領域であり、両者を混同して論じることは、誤りである。

この本来は自明であったとされる考え方が、「現代美術」という枠組みや美術館界の内側で大きく揺らぐようになってから、すでに久しい。写真家自身が意識しているといないとにかかわらず、ある種の写真は「現代美術」を指向しているとみなされ、美術評論家や美術館学芸員たちは、「現代写真」を現代美術に位置付けることにやっきになってきた。

その一方で、近年台頭めざましい日本の若手写真家の多くは、自己の出自が写真であることは前提としつつも、美術、絵画、写真、現代美術といった、固定化された旧来の美学論議などは、知らぬげである。彼ら、彼女らはアーティスト・フォトグラファーとして、伸び伸びと、華やかに、「アート・シーン」のなかで自分が表現したいものをただ表現したいように、発表することが許されている。そして、われわれは、毎日のように新たな「アート」の数々をギャラリーや美術館で発見し、愉しみ、百花繚乱の美に酔いしれている。

しかし、それらを日々追っている時、いささか会場の壁面を埋める「写真」がうるさく感じられ、観ることが疎ましくなる瞬間がある。乱舞する色彩は無秩序な豊饒としか映らなくなり、きわめて私的で、饒舌きわまりない物語性の表出は、あまりに押しつけがましく、耐え難いものとなってしまう。才能の多大なる浪費。そんな言葉すら浮かんでくる。

こうした時に、目の前のおしゃべりな「写真」の対極として思い起こされるのが、大和田良の写真である。その表現は、饒舌に対して、静謐。派手な生々しさとは無縁な、ストイックで純化された心地よい美。彼の作風を語ろうとすると、ついうっかり、大和田作品を評する際にしばしば用いられている、これら常套句が、口をついてしまいそうになる。

だが、先入観をすべて捨てて、大和田の写真一点、一点にじっくりと向かい合っていくと、柔らかな階調の光と色に彩られた一見優しげな表情は、あくまでも表面上の見かけに過ぎないことに気づき、慄然たる想いにとらわれることとなる。彼の写真は、実は手強い。

たとえば写真集『prism』に収められている作品のほとんどは、かつて写真界では「現代美術」と見なされがちであったに違いない〈World of ROUND〉シリーズの諸作を別とすれば、現実の風景や室内での日常の一コマ、あるいは花瓶に挿されたバラの花を衒いもなく、淡々ととらえたもので占められている。写しとられた情景それ自体は、われわれが生きて、呼吸をしている、「こちら側」の世界と、そうかけ離れた空間というわけではない。

なるほど、考え抜かれた構図のなかで緻密なデジタル処理が施された「世界」は、この世ならぬ、あえかな人工的色彩美に彩られてはいる。それでも風景は風景であり、子供は子供であって、大和田の作品は、写真以外の何物でもない。「スナップは自分の撮影の欲求を満たしてくれて、コンセプトのある作品は、写真とは別の思考を刺激する。両方をやっていることで、バランスが取れている部分もあると思う。ただ最終的にたどり着くのは、スナップかもしれない」という発言を信じるならば、彼の作品の根底に横たわっているのは、写真というものへの絶対的な信頼と、「写真が写真たる最も重要な要素の一つが、記録性だ」との、揺るぎない認識にあるに相違ない。大和田が、憧れの先達として、ジャック・アンリ・ラルティーグの名前を挙げるのも、けだし当然のことと納得されるのである。

ところが、そう決めてかかると、大和田の写真は、突然、観る者が内側に入り込むのを拒絶する。その際の表情は、決して優しくなどはなく、冷たく透明な強靭さに満ちている。

硬い膜が表面を覆っており、その内側からは、何の声も物音も伝わってこない。大和田の写真を初めて観たときに抱いたのは、彼の写真が写真の姿をしていながら、写真ではないかのように思えてしまった、その一瞬の戸惑いと、いわく言い難い畏れの感情であった。

そうこうするうちに、作品と抗い、押し問答を繰り返すことをあきらめると、われわれの視線はいつの間にか作品に入り込み、内側に佇んで「世界」を見つめ、感じていることに、ふと気づく。それは、厳密にいうならば、写真作品の鑑賞という行為とは異なる。撮影という理知的な「思考作業」を経たのち、綿密な構成力をもって唯一無二のプリントを仕上げていく大和田のヴィジョンに自己の視点を完全に同調させ、写真家の眼がとらえた、被写体にそなわる内的充実感と運動エネルギーを実感するという、共体験にほかならない。

いうならば大和田の眼とは、一種のレントゲン装置で、彼がとらえようとするのは、被写体の単なる外形などではなく、有機無機を問わず、事物が持つ生命力の「かたち」そのものなのである。だからこそ、〈ワイン〉シリーズが、自律した写真作品として成立することが可能になったといえるだろう。その意味からすれば、シュルレアリスム絵画に触発されたと自身で語り、制作開始初期には写真雑誌では掲載を断られたという〈World of ROUND〉シリーズもまた、うごめく自然の生命力を表現しているという点で、「スナップ」的諸作や〈ワイン〉シリーズと制作方向自体は、大きく異なるわけではなかったのである。

このような写真家・大和田良が盆栽を被写体としたならば、いったい、どのような表現世界が立ちあらわれることとなるのか。

むろんのこと、写真の本質が記録性にあるからといっても、記録する「対象」を、外観の奥底にそなわる生命力に満ちた実在感そのものと狙い定める大和田が、単なる「静物写真」としての盆栽写真を撮影するはずもない。また、盆栽写真集や盆栽展のカタログに掲載されているような一種のリアリズム写真ならば、撮影の名手は、ほかにもいるだろう。そして、なによりも、通常の美術館ならざる「美術館」を標榜する、さいたま市大宮盆栽美術館の新シリーズ〈盆栽×写真〉の第1回展である以上は、気鋭の写真家が自己の「芸術家」としてのヴィジョンをもって、館所蔵の世に知られた盆栽の名品と正面から切り結び、新たな境地を切り拓いた成果を公開する場でなくてはなるまい。かような期待と意図のもとで企画され、準備が進められたのが、このたびの新作写真展というわけである。

その結果は、ここにみるように、これまでの大和田作品からすると予想もしなかったような、意表を突くかの表現様式に従った、まことに斬新な作品群の出現であった。

考えてみれば、盆栽とは、実に不思議な「造型品」といえる。盆栽作りは、幼い苗木やそれなりに樹齢を経た山取の小さな樹木を鉢に植え、鉢の中だけで育てることからはじまる。その際に極意とされるのは、小さな素材の樹木が何十年、何百年後かに立派な盆栽へと成長し、完成した時に「この樹はこんな形、こんな姿になって欲しい」と、盆栽師が明確なイメージを自己の内に育むことにある。盆栽師はイメージを現実化していくために、樹を日々守り育てるとともに、伝統的な「型」に沿って、樹形を整える。盆栽は、その「様式美」に基づき、生きた植物を人工的な技術を駆使して造型化したものなのである。

ここ最近、「日本的なるものの見え方、見せ方」に強い関心を抱くようになったという大和田は、盆栽を「発見」した当初から、盆栽が日本の「型」の美の典型であることを紛うことなく看破していた。そして、盆栽を写真化するうえで、その一見する限りでは崩しがたい「型」を自身の表現に合わせて御していくためには、盆栽以上に強い容れものとなる枠組みが必要であるとのコンセプトを練る。そこで見出したのが、特に伝統的様式を重視する日本絵画、とりわけ装飾美と機知に富む構図を旨とした琳派の「型」に倣うことだったのである。ただし、それだけでは、絵画に憧れた「芸術写真」の二番煎じに過ぎまい。

大和田の独創性は、さらにそこに、〈World of ROUND〉シリーズで培った堅固で構成主義的な造型性を導入したことにある。いくつかに分割されて撮影された樹形は、コラージュの手法で再構築され、現実には存在しないが、一方で、あるいは存在するのかもしれないと思わせる「盆栽」の姿を、ソリッドな形で現していく。しかも、禁欲的なまでに抑制された色調は、個々の作品全体にさながら水墨画を想起させる幽玄な趣を漂わせる。そして、これらの諸要素が結びつくことで、手業の修練を重ね受け継いできた盆栽師たちの執念と、長年自由を縛られつつも、うごめく生命力を保ち続けてきた盆栽の重い想念が一体化しつつ、被写体となった実物以上に強い「盆栽」の実存感を観る者に伝えるのである。

それは、大和田芸術が新たに見せる、強靭な相貌の、まさに出発点を告げる出来事であるといえるに違いない。

Tenacious Structuralistic *Rimpa* — New *Bonsai* Photography by Ryo Ohwada

Toshiyuki Okuma Associate professor, Graduate School of Art and Design Studies at University of Toyama
The former director of the Omiya Bonsai Art Museum

Some photographic purists will say that the photograph is a photograph, not art. They will contend that photographs and paintings are totally different visual areas of expression, saying that it is the quality of the image itself that is important. The admiration for the appearance of the image continues with the argument that young photographers want to be allowed to express themselves freely, to find beautiful things in the world, without worrying about old aesthetics. The understanding of the contents of the frame are a secondary aspect compared to the visual experience. While one can be fascinated by this sense of innocent wonder that they hold, in the frame of modern art, museum biennale and the world of mass media, the power of the photograph has become much more than the explanation of personal narratives, we are looking for a new way of seeing.

Contrary to the illustrative, the works by Ryo Ohwada present us with the photograph as paradigm. I am struck in the way that his expression is just as beautiful beneath the surface as it is quiet. It is not showy with vividness, but stoic and pure, revealing a comfortable equality between his works. Still, these seem to be clichés used to make remarks on his work while the surrealist meaning of his vision remains beyond words.

When you get rid of the stereotype of beauty and take a closer look at each piece, you will find that the soft appearance of his work, characterized with gradations of light and color, is in fact superficial, and at this you will be struck delightfully with awe.

We can say that Ohwada's eyes are like a kind of X-ray machine. What he tries to observe is not the external appearance of things, but how the things exist; whether they are organic or inorganic. That is why, in the series of "Wine" works, the colors found could be said to be independent from works of photography. The "World of ROUND" series was originally refused publication by a photo magazine as a reflection of this fact. According to him, these works were inspired by surrealistic paintings, seeking to express a pure existence, more than the simple appearance of it. In this way his vision in his snapshot works and his "Wine" series are not very different from each other.

After learning this, I found that his work then takes on a surprising powerful new direction. For example, when seen in large, besides the "World of ROUND" series which has tended to be regarded as modern art, most of his works in the photo collection "prism" are not very far from the world in which we live. They consist of one observing a scene from reality, or daily life, without affection. One can see in his work that while it is true that the world processed digitally in the intended structure may only seem to be an artificial beauty, still, the scene is the scene, the children are children…

Refining the clarity of his intentions, Mr. Ohwada says that his work isn't anything but the photograph. "Snapshots satisfy my desire of shooting, and conceptual works stimulate my thoughts. Doing both of them makes me well-balanced. But finally, I believe in the snapshots." According to these words, we can tell that the basis of his work is the absolute faith in the photograph and the unshakable recognition that "the most important factor of the definition of photography is a recording." His respect for the work of Jacques-Henri Lartigue shows his dedication to this simple but encompassing truth.

Upon realizing this, his works suddenly began to refuse to let me see the artistry in them anymore. The works no longer had soft or kind looks for me, but cold and forceful ones. A rigid coat of the absolute fact of the moment covered the surface and no voice of comment or sound of abstraction came from inside. When I saw his works for the first time, I developed a nameless sense of awe in the contradiction which held me, in that, while the works conceptually were not photographs, they in fact are. What can something be when it does not appear to be what it is, especially when it is the representation itself? Could it become the moment itself?

When we give up challenging and questioning the works, however, we find ourselves standing, feeling and looking at the world from inside the photo. That is not exactly an act of viewing alone, this is an act of attuning our vision to that of Mr. Ohwada's as it works its way up through the print with his ability of structuring and shooting. Only after intellectually creating the scene conceptually, I feel, are we meant to be a part of realizing the inner contentment and motion energy in the object as it was originally observed.

So, what kind of expression appears when Ryo Ohwada takes photos of *bonsai*?

Of course, Ryo will not take the conventional still-life photos of *bonsai* trees, as his target is the reality and life beneath the surface. Why would he when there are many other good photographers who can take realistic photos of *bonsai* trees, evidenced in the abundant *bonsai* picture books and catalogs of *bonsai* exhibitions? Instead, he sees the *bonsai* as a unique artifact.

Bonsai creation begins with planting a seedling in a pot and growing it. The most important point to note is that the *bonsaishi* (*bonsai* artist) has a clear image of the future of the seedling, dreaming of the marvelous shape it will take in tens or hundreds of years in the future. The *bonsaishi* shapes and takes care of trees following the traditional styles in order to finally realize the image. Based on this stylistic beauty, the *bonsai* is a shaped living sculpture; a plant formed with conceptual skill.

As this is the 1st exhibition of the new series "Bonsai × Photography" by the Omiya Bonsai Art Museum, Ohwada is in an extraordinary situation. This photo exhibition has been designed and prepared with the intention of requiring him to confront the famed *bonsai* collection of the museum with his vision as an artist, and to present an achievement which will open up new horizons mutually.

Contrary to expectations, Ohwada emerges with an unprecedented series of works that follow a surprisingly idealistic style. These days, Ohwada says that he has been interested in the Japanese way of seeing / showing things. As soon as he discovered the form of the *bonsai*, he found that the form of each tree represents an apotheosis of Japanese stylistic beauty. Because of this, he found that, in order to photograph and to restructure this ideal through his lens he needed a rigid framework for the *bonsai*. This was a step which seemed to push against the originality of his earlier work, questioning the structuralistic way of shaping form that Ohwada originally introduced which had culminated in the "World of ROUND" series.

To break through, and to reconcile his work at the same time, Ohwada has made a marked departure. Following the style of actual traditional Japanese paintings, especially from the *rimpa* group – which are specialized in decorative and witty structures, he now takes photos of the *bonsai*, part by part, and restructures them with collage techniques. The work is fragmented to represent the *bonsai* which doesn't exist but looks real in a solid way. Stoic and understated color tones of each work remind us of the subtle and profound style of the Japanese ink painting of the *suiboku-ga*. In this tradition, the existence of the *bonsai* is highlighted more strongly than the real *bonsai* can in fact show itself. This is the surrealist in his form, bringing together the tenacity of the *bonsaishis* who have dedicated themselves to passing on the techniques and the accumulated hardships of the *bonsai* over the years, revealing the found sculpture of a tree, surviving the restraints upon its life in the pursuit of an ideal form.

In this series, Ryo Ohwada's approach has led to the fusion of photography and paintings over the living sculpture of the *bonsai*, triangulating culture, aesthetics, and the record as the composition of his vision. This must be the first step in the tenacious aspect of Ohwada's art.

真柏（A025）
白くシャリと化した細い幹が軽やかに弧を描いて伸び上がり、あたかも空にかかる橋のようである。自然の生み出した偶然の美を一鉢の中にまとめ上げた作。

The Japanese Juniper (A025)
The thin trunk with white *shari* rises curving,
and the figure looks like a bridge over the sky.
The accidental beauty of nature is in this work.

真柏（A026）
永い歳月を経て大部分が白いシャリとなった幹が見せる、ダイナミックな造型が見どころの一点。根元から枝先にかけて次第に動きを増していき、枝先では複雑にからみあった姿を見せている。

The Japanese Juniper (A026)
The characteristic of this work is the dynamic shape made
by the trunk which is very aged and has a large white *shari*.
The motion of the branches are more dynamic on the top
than on the foot, and the branches tangle complicatedly at their ends.

五葉松　銘「舞子」（A012）
本作の銘の由来である神戸市垂水区の舞子の浜は、瀬戸内の海と淡路島をのぞむ景勝地として古くから知られている。本作は根から複数の幹が立ち上った「根連なり」の樹形であり、一鉢の盆栽でありながら、風光明媚な白砂青松の舞子の浜の情景を想わせるものになっている。木々のすがたによって土地の情景を見立てた盆栽の優品である。

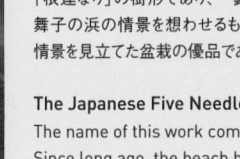

The Japanese Five Needle Pine, named "Maiko" (A012)
The name of this work comes from Maiko beach in Kobe.
Since long ago, the beach has been known as a scenic place
where you can view the Seto Inland Sea and Awajishima isle.
Several trunks are extending from the roots,
and this work shows the shape of *netsuranari* (shared roots).
In this masterpiece *bonsai*, only one tree represents the scene of
Maiko beach which has green pines on the white sandy shore.

津山檜（A028）
まっすぐに立ち上がる幹をとりまくように枝葉が層を重ねた、典型的な直幹の盆栽。津山檜は岡山県津山で発見された品種であり、葉が短く緑が濃いことから、盆栽に適した品種として好まれている。

The Japanese Cypress (A028)
This is a typical *chokkan* (straight trunk) bonsai work.
The branches and the foliage surround the straight trunk.
This cypress is called Tsuyama Cypress
as it was discovered in Tsuyama, Okayama.
This cypress has short and very green leaves and
it is liked as a tree suitable for *bonsai*.

五葉松　銘「鶴の舞」（A034）
シャリを抱えるようにねじれを帯びた幹が斜めに立ち上がり、伸びやかな動きを感じさせる一点となっている。あたかも中空で身をひるがえす鶴を想わせる姿から、「鶴の舞」という銘が付けられている。

The Japanese Five Needle Pine, named "Tsuru-no-mai" (A034)
The inclined trunk rises as if it embraces the *shari*,
and it shapes the flexible motion.
This work is named "Tsuru-no-mai (dance of a crane)"
as this looks like a crane turning its body around in the sky.

赤松　銘「帰去来」（A008）
飄々と立ち上がる細い幹と、それとは対照的に頭にのみ仕立てられた枝葉が傘を広げたように被さっている。あえて均衡を崩したかのような軽妙洒脱なつくりをした盆栽は「文人木」と呼ばれ、本作はその名品として知られている。本作の「帰去来」という銘は、中国東晋（4世紀頃）の詩人、陶淵明が宮仕えを辞め、故郷に帰る際にのこした名文である「帰去来の辞」に由来する。

The Japanese Red Pine, named "Kikyorai" (A008)
The branches and leaves are left only on the top of the slim trunk.
This kind of imbalanced bonsai is called *bunjingi*,
and this work is a famous *bunjingi* piece.
The name of the work comes from a classical Chinese poem
"The Words of Kikyorai" which Tao Yuanming wrote when he quit
his job for the dynasty and returned to his home in the 4th century.

五葉松　銘「平安」（A018）
右側へと伸びる枝の躍動感と、繁った葉のつくり出すなだらかな稜線が、静と動の絶妙な調和を見せている。力強さと端正さをあわせ持った本作には、「平安」という銘が付けられている。

The Japanese Five Needle Pine, named "Heian" (A018)
The smooth silhouette shaped by the dynamic branch growing
to the right hand and the foliage balances the stillness and motion.
The handsome and powerful work is named "Heian (peace and quiet)."

五葉松　銘「明光」（A016）
根張りからゆるやかな曲線を描いて立ち上がる幹と、左右にバランスよく配された枝が、見事な調和をみせた一点。襖絵や能舞台に描かれるような、松の理想的な姿をあらわした作となっている。

The Japanese Five Needle Pine, named "Meiko" (A016)
The winding trunk extends from the roots and the well-balanced
branches make a beatiful harmony.
This is the popular shape of pine which has appeared on
the *fusuma* screen and on the stage of *noh*.

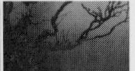

梅(月影) (A078)

古来より春の訪れを告げる梅は、盆栽としても早くから親しまれており、室町時代の絵巻物にも描かれている。歳月を重ねた幹肌が印象的な本作は、透明感のある青味をおびた白い花を咲かせる「月影」という品種である。立ち上がってひねりを加えながら大きく左に湾曲した主となる幹と、同様に湾曲した細い幹が呼応しあい、風格のある姿を形づくっている。

Tsukikage (The Japanese Apricot) (A078)

The apricot, which has told us the coming of spring since ancient times, has been popular as *bonsai* tree first appearing in an *emakimono* (scroll painting) in the Muromachi era (around 14-16C). This work is made of Tsukikage Apricot which has white blossoms with a clear bluish tone. The old skin of the trunk is very impressive. The main trunk turning left and the curved thin trunk makes a stately combination.

五葉松　銘「青龍」 (A060)

横幅が1.6メートルを超える巨体を有する本作の特徴は、その銘のとおり、龍のごとき体躯が水平にひねり伸びていく姿にある。立ち上がりから幹を縦にはしるシャリは水に濡れた龍の腹を思わせ、荒れた黒い肌は鱗を、五裂の葉は鬣や空を切る風の音を思わせる。水面にあらわれた巨龍が、天空に向けて首をもたげて昇ろうとしている姿を造型化したかのような一点である。

The Japanese Five Needle Pine, named "Seiryu" (A060)

This work named "Seiryu (blue dragon)" is over 1.6 m (5.25 ft) long, and exactly seems like a dragon turning its body horizontally. The *shari* on the base of the trunk looks like the belly of the dragon, the harsh skin seems to represent the squama, and the foliage seems like the mane or the sound of the wind. This work gorgeously expresses the shape of the great dragon flying out of the surface of the water.

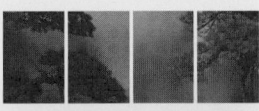

五葉松　銘「双鶴」 (A019)

大きく縦に裂け、白い断面を見せる長い幹が特徴的な一鉢。2つに割れた幹は上部で葉を繁らせ、2羽の鶴が並んでいるかのような姿をかたちづくっている。この樹形から、「双鶴」の銘が付けられた。

The Japanese Five Needle Pine, named "Sokaku" (A019)

The long trunk split vertically shows the white surface. The split trunk has foliage on the end and seems like twin cranes. The name "Sokaku (twin cranes)" was named after this form.

五葉松　銘「千尋」 (A030)

盤状に広がった厚みのある根張りには、部分的に朽ちて空洞になった「洞」が口をあけ、その上部からは白いシャリを抱えた幹がすっくと立ち上がり、樹冠部や右に伸びた枝先には青々とした葉が繁っている。はかりしれない程の長さをあらわす「千尋」という名のとおり、古代から現代へと続く、雄大な時の流れを感じさせる一点である。

The Japanese Five Needle Pine, named "Chihiro" (A030)

On the thick roots, the pine has a hollow called *uro* which has rotted away. The layered bark shows how old the tree is. On the upper part, the trunk with white *shari* comes up. Verdant five-needle leaves grow on the top and the right branch. As the name "Chihiro" means an immeasurable length, the piece expresses the grandly flowing time from anciently to the present day.

五葉松　銘「千代の松」 (A100)

本作の総高は1.6メートル、横幅は1.8メートルをこえ、大宮盆栽美術館所蔵品の中でも最大級の大きさを誇る盆栽である。土を力強くつかんで隆起した根張り、巨体をくねらせながら上昇する幹、そして量感豊かに繁った葉の威容は、樹木のたくましい生命力を感じさせる。

The Japanese Five Needle Pine, named "Chiyo-no-matsu" (A100)

This work is over 1.6m (5.2ft) high and 1.8m (6ft) wide, and is one of the biggest *bonsai* that is collected by the Omiya Bonsai Art Museum, Saitama. The roots grip the earth strongly. The trunk ascends with its body curved. The foliage grows thickly. In this way, this work shows the strength of the life of the tree.

蝦夷松 (A093)

蝦夷松の多くは北海道の千島や国後島で採られたもので、普及するのは昭和初期になってからである。独特の肌質をもった幹、小さく細かい葉の深みのある緑色など、蝦夷松には、他の松のどれとも異なる独特の魅力がある。それを寄せ植えにした本作は、大小いくつもの蝦夷松の直幹が広い大地を思わせる石盤に植えられている。左右全体の寸法が1.8メートルを超える、一鉢で蝦夷松林をあらわした大型盆栽である。

The Yezo Spruce (A093)

Many of the Yezo Spruce come from Chishima isle and Kunashiri isle and they have been famous since the early Showa period. The Yezo Spruce has appealing characteristics such as the unique skin and the deep green of the thin leaves. In this work, large and small ones are planted together on the stone board which represents the expansive ground. This is a large *bonsai* which is more than 1.8m (6ft) wide, and express a Yezo Spruce forest.

五葉松 (A102)

一抱えもある石に五葉松を根付かせた盆栽。岩肌にはもみじや長寿梅、ヤマコウバシなどが寄せ植えにされ、深山の趣を生み出している。

The Japanese Five Needle Pine (A102)

The Japanese Five Needle Pine is planted on a big stone. On the stone, the maple, the apricot and the lindera are planted together to represent the scene from deep in the mountain.

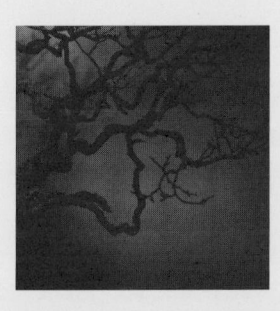

梅(思いのまま) (A079)

2本の幹がざわめくように波打ちながら枝を伸ばす姿は、さながら深山に隠れ棲む仙人の神秘的な姿を思わせる。紅白の花を咲き分ける品種「思いのまま」の一鉢。

Omoi-no-mama (The Japanese Apricot) (A079)

The rippling branches on the two trunks look like a mountain hermit who secludes himself deep in the mountain. This is Omoi-no-mama (as it likes) Apricot, which can bear the red and white blossoms as it likes.

五葉松　銘「うず潮」（A017）

本作を特徴付ける激しく渦巻いたシャリは、あたかも鉢の上にあらわれた、すさまじい海流の姿を思わせる。幹も枝も激しくねじ曲がり、枝先の葉は海流によってはじかれた波しぶきのようである。本作の迫力に満ちた姿は、自然の造型をもとに、人が永い年月をかけて手を加えたものであり、まさに盆栽が自然と人の共同制作であることを教えてくれる。

The Japanese Five Needle Pine, named "Uzushio" (A017)

The vortex-shaped *shari*, an accent of this work,
seems like a strong whirling wave.
The trunk and the branches are heavily curled,
and the leaves on the branches are like the splash of a wave.
Of course, this fantastic feature is made of nature
and has been elaborated by human hands.
That exactly represents how *bonsai* is a collaboration
between nature and mankind.

五葉松（A040）

幾つもの幹が傾きながら身を寄せ合う様が、断崖で強風に耐えながら育つ樹木の姿を想わせる作。崖を這うかのように伸びた枝が、吹きすさぶ風の強さを観る者に感じさせる。

The Japanese Five Needle Pine (A040)

Several inclined trunks huddles together to shape the tree on a cliff, surviving the strong winds. The branch following the shape of the cliff shows us how strong the wind is.

蝦夷松　銘「轟」（A005）

本作の幹は半ば空洞化しており、洞から向こう側がのぞき見えている。蝦夷松ならではの厳しい表情の樹皮の中で、シャリが一際白い輝きを放っており、鳴り響く雷のような激しい音を意味する「轟」という銘にふさわしい姿を見せている。

The Yezo Spruce, named "Todoroki" (A005)

This work has a hollow, through which we can see the other side.
The white shari stands out on the hard skin of the Yezo Spruce.
This work is named "Todoroki" which means the sound of
the rolling thunder.

五葉松　銘「白雲」（A006）

立ち上がった幹が鋭い角度で下方へ折り返した、懸崖の作。上方からおりてきた枝の先に繁った葉が層を重ね、渓谷をたゆとう霞を想わせる本作には、「白雲」という銘が付けられている。

The Japanese Five Needle Pine, named "Hakuun" (A006)

This is a kind of *kengai* (tree-on-cliff) work.
The raised trunk turns sharply downward.
The leaves on the end of the declining branch make a layerd foliage,
which looks like mist flowing around the cliff.
The name "Hakuun" means white cloud.

五葉松（A043）

自然の風向きによって一方向に幹が流れている木の姿をあらわした「吹流し」の樹形の作。4本の幹が傾斜しながら層をなし、険しい山岳で強風に耐える情景を想わせる。

The Japanese Five Needle Pine (A043)

This work represents a tree inclined in one direction by the force of the natural wind. This shape is called *fukinagashi*.
The four inclined trunks represents the tree surviving the strong wind on the steep mountain.

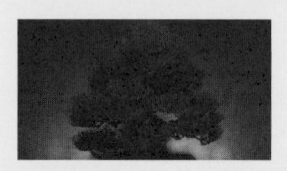

黒松（A064）

安定感のあるどっしりとした根元と、歳月を重ねた荒々しい肌が、黒松ならではの力強い生命力や、大樹の風格を感じさせる。バランスよく配された枝が、端整な趣を形づくる一点。

The Black Pine (A064)

The stately roots and the aged skin shows the powerful vitality of the Black Pine and the dignity of a big tree.
The well-balanced branches gives a handsome character.

五葉松　銘「日暮し」（A001）

五葉松の名高い作品であり、戦前に新潟の石油王として知られた中野忠太郎が所蔵していた折に、一日見ていても飽きないという意味を込めて「日暮し」という銘が付けられた。大小ふたつの幹の間に抱えこまれるようにして生まれた空間が、不思議な魅力をもって鑑賞者の視線を引き寄せる。なお本作は年月をかけて両面から作りこまれているため、どちらを正面にしても鑑賞できるつくりとなっている。

The Japanese Five Needle Pine, named "Higurashi" (A001)

This is a renowned Five Needle Pine *bonsai* work kept by Chutaro Nakano who was known as an oil magnate in Niigata before WWII.
This work was named "Higurashi", which implies that we won't be tired of looking at it even if we look at it all day long.
The space embraced by the two thick and thin trunks
fascinates the viewer and draws their gaze.
This work has been elaborated from both sides over a long time,
so you can view it in the round.

五葉松　銘「白糸の滝」（A003）

本作は、険しい崖に風雪に耐えながら根付いた木の姿をあらわした、「懸崖」と呼ばれる樹形に仕立てられている。根元は鉢を覆うように隆起し、そこから下方へと伸びる白肌の枝は、幾筋もの流れ落ちる水流を想わせる。「白糸の滝」という銘にふさわしく、雄大な滝の姿に見立てられた懸崖樹の逸品である。

The Japanese Five Needle Pine, named "Shiraito-no-taki" (A003)

This work is made into the shape called *kengai* (tree-on-cliff),
which represents the tree taking root on a steep cliff
and living in hard wind and rain.
The raised roots cover the pot, and the descending white branches
evoke the image of strands of waterfalls.
The leaves on the end of the branch seem like
a falling splash or a ripple on the surface.
Worthy of the name "Shiraito-no-taki (white waterfall)",
it's a gem of a *kengai* work resembling a magnificent waterfall.

大和田良

1978年仙台市生まれ
日本在住

2002　東京工芸大学芸術学部写真学科卒業
2004　東京工芸大学大学院芸術学研究科メディアアート専攻修了

2004　写真家集団 "StairAUG." 発足
2010　東京工芸大学芸術学部写真学科非常勤講師

主な個展
2011　FORM　さいたま市大宮盆栽美術館／埼玉
2010　Log.　キヤノンギャラリー／東京、梅田、名古屋、札幌、仙台、福岡
　　　ノーツ オン フォトグラフィー　B GALLERY／新宿
　　　wine collection　EMON PHOTO GALLERY／広尾
2009　大和田良個展　西武渋谷店 プラチナサロン／渋谷
2007　Strings of Life　B GALLERY／新宿
　　　prism　nano-universe／渋谷
2005　ID　アートフォトサイト／目黒
　　　SOURCE　ニコンサロン／新宿、大阪
2003　World of ROUND　コニカミノルタプラザ／新宿

主なグループ展
2011　SAKURA　MICHEKO GALERIE／ミュンヘン
2010　10's aqua green　EMON PHOTO GALLERY／広尾
2009　reGeneration 50 photographers of tomorrow　プレウス美術館／ホーテン（ノルウェー）
　　　y-Generation　西武渋谷店／渋谷
2008　コンテンポラリーアートフェア～シブヤスタイル　西武渋谷店／渋谷
　　　StairAUG.photographics S/S　B GALLERY／新宿
　　　StairAUG.photographics A/W　Therme gallery／目黒
2007　reGeneration 50 photographers of tomorrow　アリス・ド・ルーレット・ウィリアムソンギャラリー／カリフォルニア
　　　Making, Marking, Mapping　PGI／芝浦
2006　Kunst RAI　ライ・パークホール／アムステルダム
　　　reGeneration 50 photographers of tomorrow　アパチャー／ニューヨーク
　　　First Sight - Neuheiten aus dem Portfolio　ルマスギャラリー／ベルリン
2005　reGeneration 50 fotografi di domani　ガレリア カルラ・ソッツァーニ／ミラノ
　　　reGeneration 50 photographers of tomorrow　エリゼ美術館／ローザンヌ（スイス）
2004　StairAUG.photographics　コニカミノルタプラザ新宿、PROSPER TOKYO／代官山
2003　TPCC受賞記念展　東京写真文化館／赤坂

主な受賞歴
2011　日本写真協会賞 新人賞
2005　reGeneration 50 photographers of tomorrow　エリゼ美術館／ローザンヌ（スイス）
2004　ニコン ユーナ21
2003　コニカミノルタフォトプレミオ
　　　フォックスタルボット賞

出版
2010　『ノーツ オン フォトグラフィー』（リブロアルテ）
2007　『prism』（青幻舎）

作品収蔵
エリゼ美術館、東京工芸大学

Ryo OHWADA

Born in Sendai, Japan. 1978.
Lives in Tokyo.

2002　Graduated from Department of Photography at Tokyo Polytechnic University.
2004　Finished Graduate School of Arts at Tokyo Polytechnic University (majored in the media art studies).

2004　Founded the organization of photographers "StairAUG."　http://www.stairaug.com/
2010-　Assistant professor, Department of Photography at Tokyo Polytechnic University

Major Solo Exhibitions
2011　FORM at the Omiya Bonsai Art Museum, Saitama
2010　Notes on Photography at B GALLERY, Tokyo
　　　Log. at Canon Gallery, Tokyo and 5 other cities in Japan
　　　wine collection at EMON PHOTO GALLERY, Tokyo
2009　Ryo OHWADA Solo Exhibition at Shibuya Seibu, Tokyo
2007　Strings of Life at B GALLERY, Tokyo
　　　prism at nano-universe, Tokyo
2005　ID at Art Photo Site, Tokyo
　　　SOURCE at Nikon salon, Tokyo and Osaka
2003　World of ROUND at Konica Minorta Plaza, Tokyo

Major Group Exhibitions
2011　SAKURA at MICHEKO GALLERY, Munich
2010　10's aqua green at EMON PHOTO GALLERY, Tokyo
2009　reGeneration 50 photographers of tomorrow at Preus Museum, Horten, Norway
　　　y-Generation at Shibuya Seibu, Tokyo
2008　Contemporary Art Fair -Shibuya Style- at Shibuya Seibu, Tokyo
　　　StairAUG.photographics S/S at B GALLERY, Tokyo
　　　StairAUG.photographics A/W at Therme Gallery, Tokyo
2007　reGeneration 50 photographers of tomorrow at Alyce de Roulet Williamson Gallery, California
　　　Making, Marking, Mapping at PGI, Tokyo
2006　Kunst RAI at RAI Park Hall, Amsterdam
　　　reGeneration 50 photographers of tomorrow at Aperture, New York
　　　First Sight - Neuheiten aus dem Portfolio at Lumas Gallery, Berlin
2005　reGeneration 50 fotografi di domani at Galleria CARLA SOZZANI, Milano
　　　reGeneration 50 photographers of tomorrow at Musée de l'Elysée, Lausannne, Switzerland
　　　StairAUG.photographics at Konica Minorta Plaza and PROSPER TOKYO, Tokyo
2003　Exhibition for TPCC Award at Tokyo Photographic Culture Center, Tokyo

Major Grants and Awards
2011　Newcomer's Award of Photographic Society of Japan Awards
2005　reGeneration 50 photographers of tomorrow, Musée de l'Elysée, Lausanne, Switzerland
2004　Nikon Juna21
2003　Konica Minorta FOTO PREMIO
　　　Fox Talbot Award

Publication
2010　"Notes on Photography" LibroArte., Inc.
2007　"prism" SEIGENSHA, Ltd.

Public Collection
Musée de l'Elysée, Tokyo Polytechnic University

FORM – SCENERY SEEN THROUGH BONSAI

2011年5月21日　初版発行

著者　大和田良

企画　田中廉也(株式会社モデルノ)
協力・解説　さいたま市大宮盆栽美術館

アートディレクション&デザイン　吉田ナオヤ(株式会社深水社)
翻訳　Jeremiah Magone　岩崎元気
プリンティングディレクター　井上 優(凸版印刷株式会社)

発行者　大澤弘子
発行所　株式会社深水社　ShinSuiSha Publishing
　　　　160-0022　東京都新宿区新宿1-5-13-3F
TEL　03-5369-0271
FAX　03-5369-0272
　　　　http://www.shinsuisha.com
印刷・製本　凸版印刷株式会社

©2011 Ryo Ohwada / ShinSuiSha Inc. ShinSuiSha Publishing

Printed in Japan
ISBN978-4-9905818-0-0
乱丁・落丁本はお取り替えいたします。本書の無断複写・複製・転載・引用を禁じます。

FORM – SCENERY SEEN THROUGH BONSAI

Ryo Ohwada
First Edition: May 21, 2011

Planning: Renya Tanaka (Moderno Co.,Ltd.)
Support: The Omiya Bonsai Museum, Saitama

Art Direction&Design: Naoya Yoshida (ShinSuiSha Inc.)
Translation: Jeremiah Magone　Motoki Iwasaki
Printing Director: Masaru Inoue

Publisher: Hiroko Osawa
Publishing Office: ShinSuiSha Inc. ShinSuiSha Publishing
1-5-13-3F Shinjuku, Shinjuku-ku, Tokyo 160-0022 Japan
TEL: +81-3-5369-0271
FAX: +81-3-5369-0272
http://www.shinsuisha.com
Printed and bound by Toppan Printing Co.,Ltd.

©2011 Ryo Ohwada / ShinSuiSha Inc. ShinSuiSha Publishing

Printed in Japan
ISBN978-4-9905818-0-0
All rights reserved.
No part of this book may be reproduced or transmitted in any form or by any means,
electronic or mechanical, including photocopying, recording or by any information storage and retrieval system,
without permission in writing from the publisher.

SHIN SUI SHA PUBLISHING